# African Animals

# Hippopotamuses

Big Buddy BOOKS
African Animals

by Julie Murray

ABDO
Publishing Company

**VISIT US AT**
**www.abdopublishing.com**

Published by ABDO Publishing Company, PO Box 398166, Minneapolis, MN 55439.

Printed in the United States of America, North Mankato, Minnesota.
102011
012012

♻ PRINTED ON RECYCLED PAPER

Coordinating Series Editor: Rochelle Baltzer
Editor: Marcia Zappa
Contributing Editors: Megan M. Gunderson, BreAnn Rumsch, Sarah Tieck
Graphic Design: Maria Hosley
Cover Photograph: *Shutterstock*: Todd Hackwelder.
Interior Photographs/Illustrations: *Animals Animals - Earth Scenes*: ©Ardea/Labat, Ferrero (pp. 23, 26, 29),
©Osf/Downer, John (p. 16), ©Wegner, Jorg & Petra (p. 25); *iStockphoto*: ©iStockphoto.com/africa924 (p. 9),
©iStockphoto.com/brytta (p. 4), ©iStockphoto.com/bucky_za (p. 21), ©iStockphoto.com/CraigRJD
(pp. 7, 12, 21), ©iStockphoto.com/elfart (p. 9), ©iStockphoto.com/GlobalP (p. 12), ©iStockphoto.com/
JohnDPorter (p. 8), ©iStockphoto.com/lcaizlova (p. 19), ©iStockphoto.com/Lingbeek (p. 11), ©iStockphoto.com/
namibelephant (p. 24), ©iStockphoto.com/pjmalsbury (pp. 7, 15), ©iStockphoto.com/prill (p. 8), ©iStockphoto.
com/PTB-images (p. 4); *JohnFoxx Images* (p. 5); *Shutterstock*: hallam creations (p. 25), CHENGYUAN YANG
(p. 13); *Stockbyte* (p. 9).

**Library of Congress Cataloging-in-Publication Data**

Murray, Julie, 1969-
Hippopotamuses / Julie Murray.
    p. cm. -- (African animals)
ISBN 978-1-61783-220-8
1. Hippopotamidae--Juvenile literature.  I. Title.
QL737.U57M87 2012
599.63'5--dc23
                                                    2011031041

# Contents

Long ago, nearly all land on Earth was one big mass. About 200 million years ago, the land began to break into **continents**. One of these is Africa.

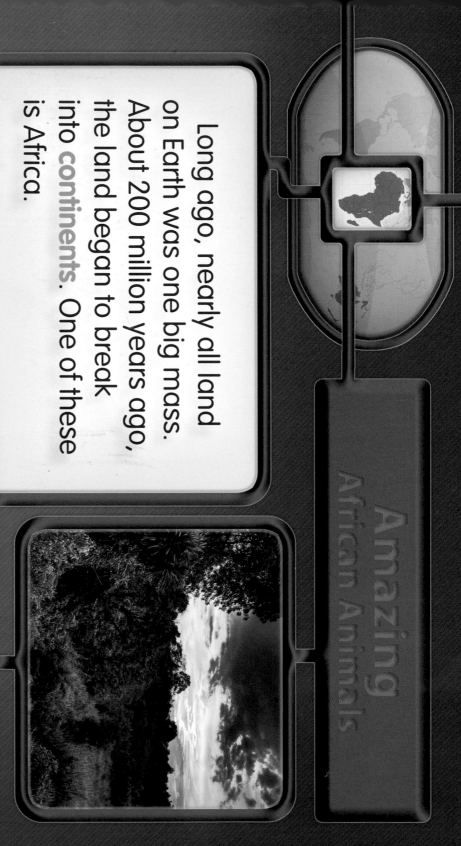

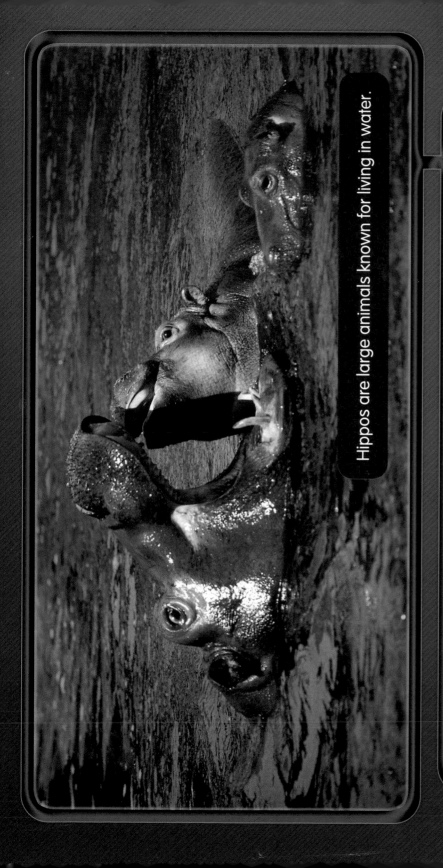

Hippos are large animals known for living in water.

Africa is the second-largest **continent**. It is known for hot weather, wild land, and interesting animals. One of these animals is the hippopotamus, or hippo. In the wild, hippos are found only in Africa.

# Hippopotamus Territory

There are two types of hippos. These are the river hippo and the pygmy (PIHG-mee) hippo.

River hippos are found across central Africa's open grasslands. They live in lakes, rivers, and streams.

Pygmy hippos are found in small areas of western Africa. They live in thick forests near streams.

SAHARA DESERT

Nile River

▦ River Hippo Territory
▨ Pygmy Hippo Territory

Pygmy hippos are very uncommon. So, scientists still have much to learn about them.

River hippos are also called common hippos and Nile hippos.

# Jambo! Welcome to Africa!

If you took a trip to where hippopotamuses live, you might find...

## ...the world's longest river.

The Nile River flows more than 4,000 miles (6,400 km)! It stretches from east-central Africa north to the Mediterranean Sea. Many river hippos live in the southern part of the Nile.

## ...few forests.

Forests are not very common in Africa. They cover less than one-fifth of the continent. Where forests do grow, they are often thick, wet rain forests. Many uncommon animals live in these habitats. They include forest elephants, gorillas, and pygmy hippos.

## ...many languages.

More than 1,000 languages are spoken across Africa! Swahili (swah-HEE-lee) is common in central Africa where river hippos live. In Swahili, *jambo* is a greeting for visitors. *Masalala* means "goodness!" or "wow!" And, *kiboko* means "hippopotamus."

## ...villages.

Villages are common in central Africa. Small villages are often made up of a group of homes surrounded by farms. Larger villages may include a school, a courthouse, or a few shops. People living in villages often form close communities.

# Take a Closer Look

River hippos are huge. They weigh from 2,500 to 8,000 pounds (1,100 to 3,600 kg) or more! River hippos are about 5 feet (1.5 m) tall at their shoulders. And, they are 11 to 16 feet (3.4 to 4.9 m) long.

Pygmy hippos are much smaller than river hippos. They weigh just 350 to 600 pounds (160 to 270 kg). Pygmy hippos stand 2.5 to 3 feet (0.8 to 0.9 m) tall. And, they are 5 to 6 feet (1.5 to 1.8 m) long.

River hippos are among the heaviest land animals. Only certain elephants and rhinoceroses weigh more.

Hippos have long, round bodies and short legs. They have thick, mostly smooth skin.

A hippo has a large head and **snout**. It has big teeth, including **tusks**. But, its eyes and ears are small.

A river hippo's skin is brownish-gray or grayish-purple (*left*). A pygmy hippo's skin is grayish-black (*below*).

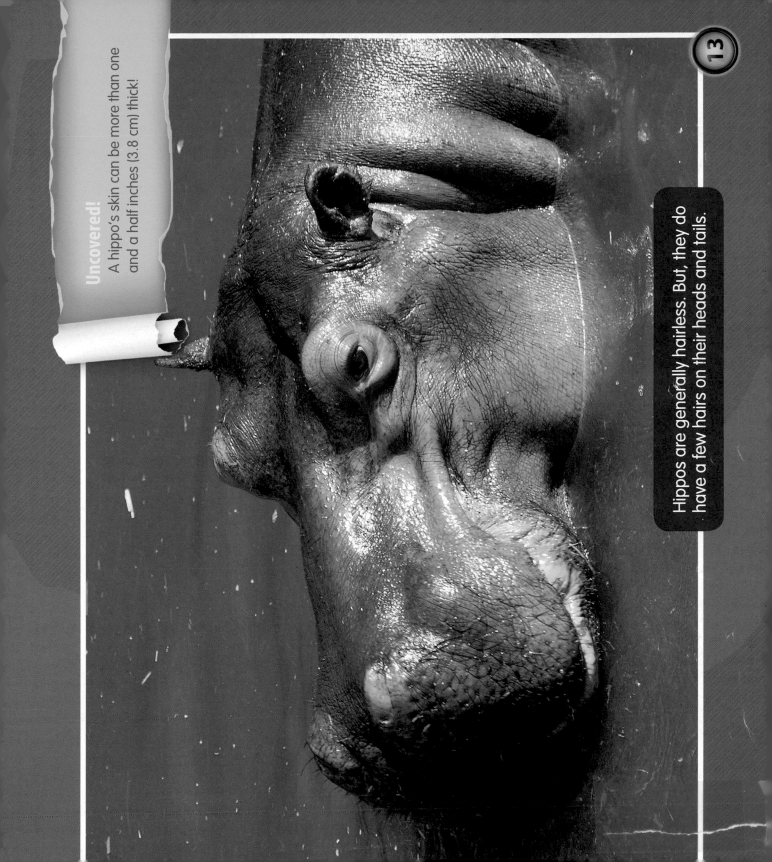

**Uncovered!**
A hippo's skin can be more than one and a half inches (3.8 cm) thick!

Hippos are generally hairless. But, they do have a few hairs on their heads and tails.

# Watery Days

Hippos spend their days resting and sleeping in water. This helps them stay cool in the hot African sun.

Hippos are well built for life in water. Their eyes, ears, and noses are high on their heads. This lets them see, hear, and breathe while mostly underwater.

Sometimes, hippos go all the way underwater. Their noses and ears close tightly so no water gets in.

A hippo's head and back often stick out of the water like little islands. Birds, turtles, and even baby crocodiles sometimes sit on them!

Adult hippos don't swim the way most
water animals do. Their bodies are so
heavy that they can sink to the bottom.
Then, they move through water by taking
long, springy steps.

**Uncovered!**
Hippos have very thin sheets of skin covering
their eyes. These guard their eyes while still
allowing them to see underwater.

Adult hippos can hold their breath underwater for about five minutes!

17

# Mealtime

At night, hippos leave the water to eat. Hippos are **herbivores**. They eat grass, fruit, and leaves. River hippos try to stay close to water while they eat. But sometimes, they must walk as far as five miles (8 km) to find food!

River hippos eat 80 to 150 pounds (40 to 70 kg) of food each night. This may sound like a lot. But, it is actually a small amount compared to their size.

A hippo's wide snout helps it collect many plants in each bite.

# Social Life

River hippos are **social** animals. They live in groups of 5 to 30. Groups have several males, females, and young. Each group is led by one **dominant** male.

The dominant male controls the group's territory and females. He may **mate** with all the females in the group. Sometimes, he allows other males to mate as well.

**Uncovered!**
A dominant male hippo marks his territory with his poop. He uses his tail to throw it as far as possible.

Pygmy hippos live alone or in pairs. They spend more time on land than river hippos do.

A group of hippos is called a herd, a bloat, a pod, or a siege.

Male hippos **compete** to be the **dominant** male in a group. First, they open their mouths three to four feet (0.9 to 1.2 m) wide. This shows off their large **tusks**. Usually, this is enough to scare away a smaller male.

Other times, male hippos fight. They swing their large heads and try to cut each other with their tusks. These fights often cause deep wounds, broken bones, and even death.

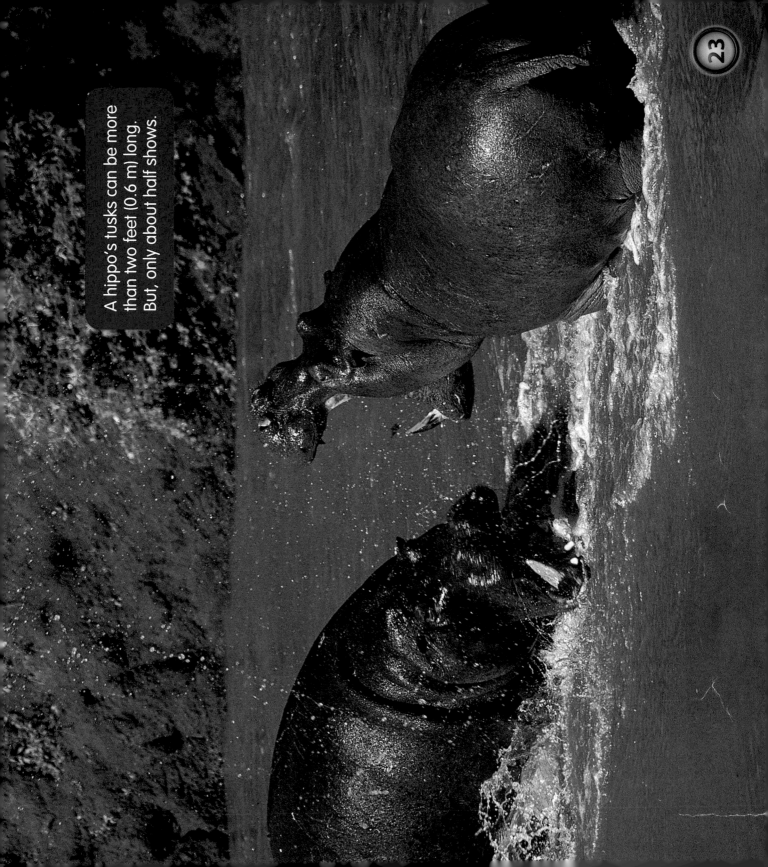

A hippo's tusks can be more than two feet (0.6 m) long. But, only about half shows.

# Baby Hippos

Hippos are **mammals**. Female hippos usually have one baby at a time. Baby hippos are called calves. River hippo calves are often born underwater! They can swim just moments after they are born.

**Uncovered!**
Pygmy hippo calves are usually born on land.

At birth, many river hippo calves already weigh about 100 pounds (45 kg)!

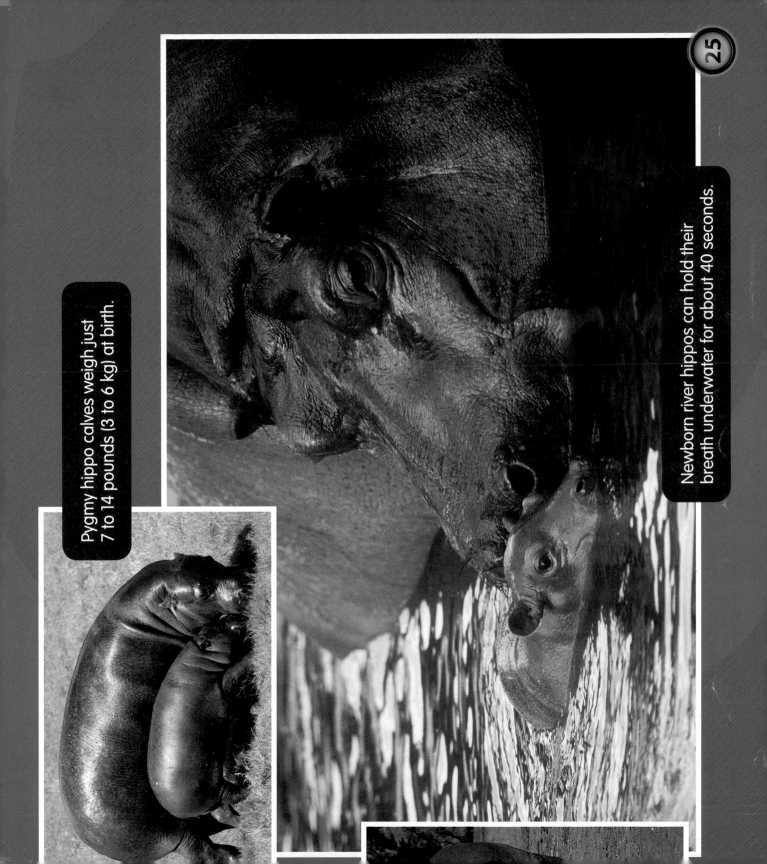

Pygmy hippo calves weigh just 7 to 14 pounds (3 to 6 kg) at birth.

Newborn river hippos can hold their breath underwater for about 40 seconds.

Predators rarely attack adult hippos. But calves are hunted by lions, crocodiles, hyenas, and leopards. So, they stay close to their mothers. This is very important when they are on land searching for food and eating.

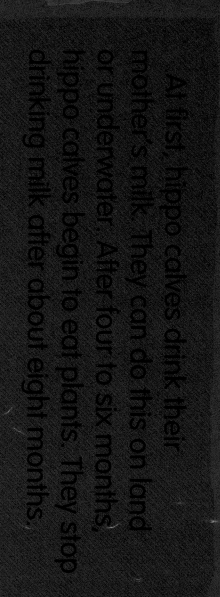

At first, hippo calves drink their mother's milk. They can do this on land or underwater. After four to six months, hippo calves begin to eat plants. They stop drinking milk after about eight months.

A hippo calf often rests on its mother's back in the water.

# Survivors

Life in Africa isn't easy for hippos. New farms take over their **habitats**. Their watery homes are becoming polluted. Farmers kill hippos that eat or walk on their crops. And, people hunt hippos for their meat and ivory **tusks**.

Still, hippos **survive**. In the wild, they live 30 to 40 years. Hippopotamuses help make Africa an amazing place!

**Uncovered!**
River hippos are vulnerable. This means they are in some danger of dying out. Pygmy hippos are endangered. This means they are in great danger of dying out.

River hippos are very forceful and do not fear humans. They are considered one of the most dangerous animals in Africa!

# Masala!

## I'll bet you never knew...

...that the name *hippopotamus* comes from the Greek words for "river horse." But, hippos are not in the same animal family as horses. Hippos are related to pigs, whales, and dolphins.

...that hippos sweat blood. Not really! But for a long time people thought they did. A river hippo's skin oozes an oily pink or red liquid. It keeps the skin from getting too dry. And, it guards against the hot African sun.

...that many scientists believe humans should raise hippos as farm animals. For their size, hippos provide a lot of meat compared to other African animals. And, hippo meat is very healthy to eat.

# Important Words

**compete** to take part in a contest between two or more animals, persons, or groups.

**continent** one of Earth's seven main land areas.

**dominant** commanding or controlling all others.

**habitat** a place where a living thing is naturally found.

**herbivore** (HUHR-buh-vawr) an animal that eats plants.

**mammal** a member of a group of living beings. Mammals make milk to feed their babies and usually have hair or fur on their skin.

**mate** to join as a couple in order to reproduce, or have babies.

**snout** a part of the face, including the nose and the mouth, that sticks out. Some animals, such as hippopotamuses, have a snout.

**social** (SOH-shuhl) naturally living or growing in groups.

**survive** to continue to live or exist.

**tusks** large, long teeth that stick out of an animal's mouth.

# Web Sites

To learn more about hippopotamuses, visit ABDO Publishing Company online. Web sites about hippopotamuses are featured on our Book Links page. These links are routinely monitored and updated to provide the most current information available.

**www.abdopublishing.com**

# Index